People of the World

Multicultural Projects and Activities

 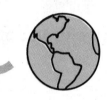 

Written by Denise Bieniek

Illustrated by Paige Billin-Frye

Troll Early Learning Activities

Troll Early Learning Activities is a classroom-tested series designed to provide time-pressured teachers with a wide range of theme-related projects and activities to enhance lesson plans and enrich the curriculum. Each book focuses on a different area of early childhood learning, from math and writing to art and science. Using a wide range of activities, each title in this series is chockful of innovative ideas, handy reproducible pages, puzzles and games, classroom projects, suggestions for bulletin boards and learning centers, and much more.

With highly interactive student projects and teacher suggestions that make learning fun, Troll Early Learning Activities is an invaluable classroom resource you'll turn to again and again. We hope you will enjoy using the worksheets and activities presented in these books. And we know your students will benefit from the dynamic, creative learning environment you have created!

Titles in this series:

Animal Friends: Projects and Activities for Grades K-3

Circle Time Fun: Projects and Activities for Grades Pre-K-2

Classroom Decorations: Ideas for a Creative Classroom

Early Literacy Skills: Projects and Activities for Grades K-3

Helping Hands: Small Motor Skills Projects and Activities

Hi, Neighbor! Projects and Activities About Our Community

Number Skills: Math Projects and Activities for Grades K-3

People of the World: Multicultural Projects and Activities

Our World: Science Projects and Activities for Grades K-3

Seasons and Holidays: Celebrations All Year Long

Story Time: Skill-Building Projects and Activities for Grades K-3

Time, Money, Measurement: Projects and Activities Across the Curriculum

---

Metric Conversion Chart

1 inch = 2.54 cm	1 foot = .305 m	1 yard = .914 m
1 mile = 1.61 km	1 fluid ounce = 29.573 ml	1 cup = .24 l
1 pint = .473 l	1 teaspoon = 4.93 ml	1 tablespoon = 14.78 ml

Contents

Houses Around the World

What kind of house do you live in? Discuss the different kinds of housing shown here, and then color the one that best matches your home.

On the back, draw a picture of the house you would someday like to live in.

Paper Dolls

1. Explain to the class that long ago, when travel was much more difficult, people rarely met anyone from far away, and people wore clothing similar to that of their neighbors. As travel became easier, clothing styles spread throughout the world. Fabric was shipped to different countries.

2. Tell children that in modern times, people in one part of the world can dress like people in other parts of the world. People in America may wear kimonos, a type of clothing that originated in Japan.

3. Ask students if they can think of any styles of clothing that have faded from popularity (and perhaps returned years later), such as bell bottoms and miniskirts.

4. Reproduce the dolls on this page and the traditional clothing on pages 7, 8, and 9 once for each student. Have students color the patterns, mount them on oaktag, and cut them out. If desired, laminate the patterns.

5. Help students research traditional dress in other countries. Ask them to draw pictures of people wearing traditional dress. Display the pictures on a bulletin board under the title "Clothing—What's Your Style?"

Traditional Clothing

Japan

Traditional Clothing

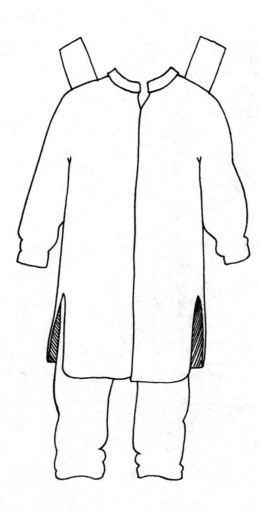

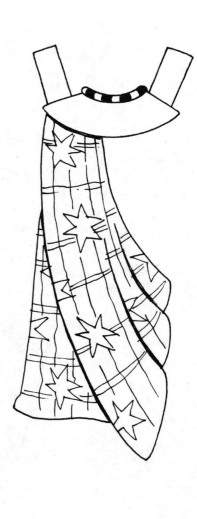

India

India

Africa

Traditional Clothing

Africa

Pioneer America

My Own Recipe Book

Materials:

- scissors
- lined paper
- glue
- construction paper
- crayons or markers
- oaktag
- clear contact paper
- hole puncher
- yarn

Directions:

1. Reproduce the art on page 11 once for each child. Have children color the covers and cut them out.

2. Mount each cover on a 9" x 12" piece of oaktag.

3. Ask children to gather simple recipes from family and friends. Encourage students to find out what type of cuisine (e.g., Italian, Mexican) each recipe belongs to, and from where the foods that make up each recipe originate.

4. Have students write each recipe on lined paper and then glue the recipe onto a 9" x 12" piece of construction paper.

5. When each child is satisfied with the number of recipes he or she has collected, have him or her place the cover on top of the recipes. Then punch three holes along the left side of the book, as shown.

6. Tie short lengths of yarn through each hole to bind the pages of the book.

7. Ask each student to write the name of the country from which each recipe originated on the facing page.

8. Place the books in the classroom reading center. Students may wish to add more recipes to their books before taking them home.

My Own Recipe Book

Best Books

Share some of the multicultural books below with the class. Discuss the ways in which the cultures and experiences in the books are similar and different from those of the students in the class.

The Festival by Peter Bonnici (Carolrhoda, 1985)

Apple Pie and Onions by Judith Caseley (Greenwillow, 1987)

The Art Lesson by Tomie de Paola (Putnam, 1989)

Everybody Cooks Rice by Norah Dooley (Carolrhoda, 1992)

How My Parents Learned to Eat by Ina Friedman (Houghton Mifflin, 1984)

Family Pictures by Carmen Lomas Garza (Children's Book Press, 1990)

Family Scrapbook by M. B. Goffstein (Farrar, Straus, 1978)

Tell Me a Story, Mama by Angela Johnson (Franklin Watts, 1989)

How My Family Lives in America by Susan Kuklin (Bradbury Press, 1992)

My Little Island by Frané Lessac (HarperCollins, 1985)

Leo the Late Bloomer by Leo Lionni (Simon & Schuster, 1971)

The Balancing Girl by Berniece Rabe (Dutton, 1988)

People by Peter Spier (Doubleday 1980)

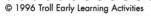

Hello! Around the World

Materials:

- blue bulletin board paper
- world map
- stapler
- scraps of oaktag
- markers
- thumbtacks
- 3" x 5" index cards
- glue

Directions:

1. Cover a bulletin board with blue paper. Staple a world map in the center of the board.

2. Choose ten countries on the map and ask volunteers to make a small country flag for each country on 2" x 3" pieces of oaktag.

3. On the front of each flag, using a black marker, write a number from one to ten. Pin the flags to the board in the appropriate spots.

4. On 3" x 5" index cards, write the word(s) for "Hello" in the languages of the ten countries chosen. Place a blank index card under each hello card and glue across the top so they are closed only along the top. On the bottom card, write the number of the country that matches the "Hello" written on the front card.

5. Arrange these cards randomly around the bulletin board, stapling along the top. Then staple the bottom of the back cards to the board.

6. To play the "Hello" activity, have students read the "Hello" in each language, then try to guess in which country it is spoken. To check themselves, students may lift the top card and read the number underneath. They can look at the map to discover which country says "Hello" that way.

Schools Around the World

1. Have a class discussion about the different types of schools in the world. Explain that children attend school everywhere in the world. What varies in each place is the length of the school day and year, the subjects the children learn, what type of building the school is housed in, the daily schedule, and the extracurricular activities.

2. Name some places and show the children the area where they live on a map. Ask them to imagine what it would be like to go to school in a hot place, a cold place, a place by a river, a place high up in the mountains, or a place in the country. Then share the following facts about students in other countries with the class.

In Khabura, Oman, children did not have a school to go to until 1970, when Sultan Qaboos became the ruler of Oman and had many schools built. The school is a concrete building with wooden desks in rows. Two students sit at each desk. Children sometimes use donkeys to ride to school.

In France, children go to school at about 8:30 in the morning. Younger children go to a primary school and older children attend a secondary school, or *lycee*. Most schoolchildren go home for lunch. They eat and spend some time on homework or other activities before they go back to school for the afternoon. French children go to school on Saturday mornings and have Wednesday afternoons free.

In a small town called Siorapaluk in Greenland, the church is used as the school on weekdays. All the children between the ages of 7 and 12 years old go to school there. Some children are sent to a school about 50 miles away to continue their educations. The school year is over at the end of May and begins in August.

3. Borrow books from the library about schools and schooling in other cultures and have students compare and contrast the experiences of children in other cultures with their own.

4. Give each student a sheet of paper and demonstrate how to fold it in half. On one side, ask each child to draw a picture of his or her life at school. On the other side, ask students to draw pictures of schools in other cultures, showing how it is different from or similar to their own.

5. Gather the pages together and place a blank piece of paper on top to make a cover. Punch three holes along the left side.

6. Bind the pages together with yarn to make a class book. Have the class brainstorm to come up with a title for their book.

Toys Around the World

In the imaginary country of Doodlemond, the unit of money used is called the "doodle." Convert the price for each of the items below from doodles into dollars. Write the dollar amount on the line provided.

$1 = 20 doodles

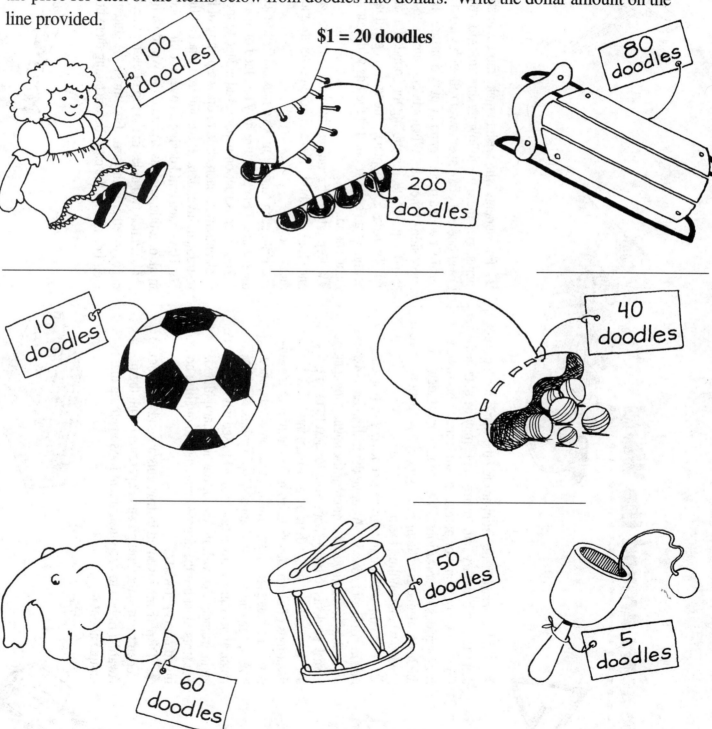

100 doodles

200 doodles

80 doodles

10 doodles

40 doodles

60 doodles

50 doodles

5 doodles

Instruments Around the World

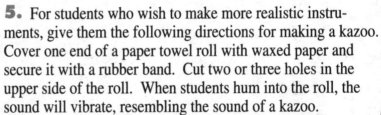

1. Collect instruments from around the world for the students to touch and try out. Instruments may be obtained from the school band or parents of students, or borrowed from various organizations. (Before inviting students to try the instruments, give them a few guidelines about the care needed when handling them.)

2. Encourage children to experiment with instruments making different sounds. Arrange the instruments in a line on a table according to the pitch of the sound they make. Or ask students to order them from loudest to most quiet.

3. Let students make their own instruments. Ask for donations of clean materials from the families of the students, such as paper towel rolls, juice containers, shoe boxes, egg cartons, wire hangers, and jar lids. Hold a musical instrument invention contest to see who can create an instrument that will make noise when manipulated. Students must use the donated materials to qualify; no real instruments allowed.

4. Display the invented instruments around the room so students can walk through and experiment with them. Award a ribbon to each instrument for something that is unique about it.

5. For students who wish to make more realistic instruments, give them the following directions for making a kazoo. Cover one end of a paper towel roll with waxed paper and secure it with a rubber band. Cut two or three holes in the upper side of the roll. When students hum into the roll, the sound will vibrate, resembling the sound of a kazoo.

6. To make a xylophone, glue various-sized jar lids to the bottom of an egg carton. Hit the lids with a drum stick or a metal spoon.

7. Reproduce the musical instrument art on pages 17 and 18 once for each child. Have children color the pictures and cut them out.

8. Help each student make a musical instruments book using the pictures. Each picture may be glued onto a bright piece of oaktag or construction paper. Add a page to the end of each book and invite each child to draw a picture of his or her own instrument invention. Have children label all the pictures.

9. Have each child design a cover for his or her book and think of a title, such as "Around the World with Music."

10. Punch two holes in the top of each page. Bind the pages together with yarn. Encourage the students to share their books with the class before taking them home.

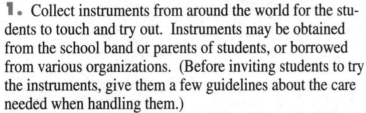
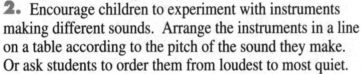

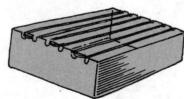

Instruments Around the World

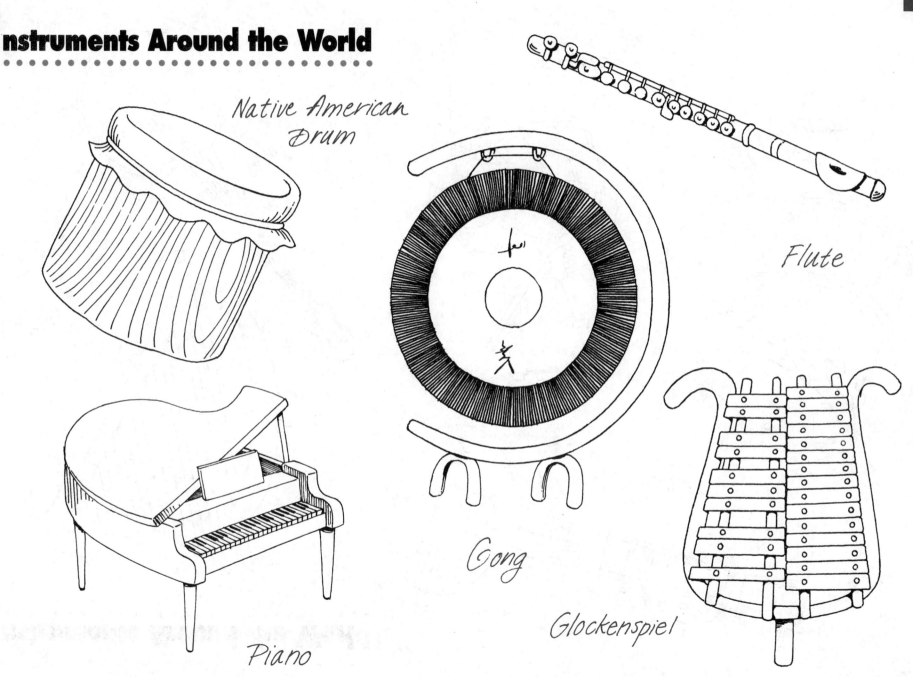

Native American Drum

Flute

Gong

Piano

Glockenspiel

Instruments Around the World

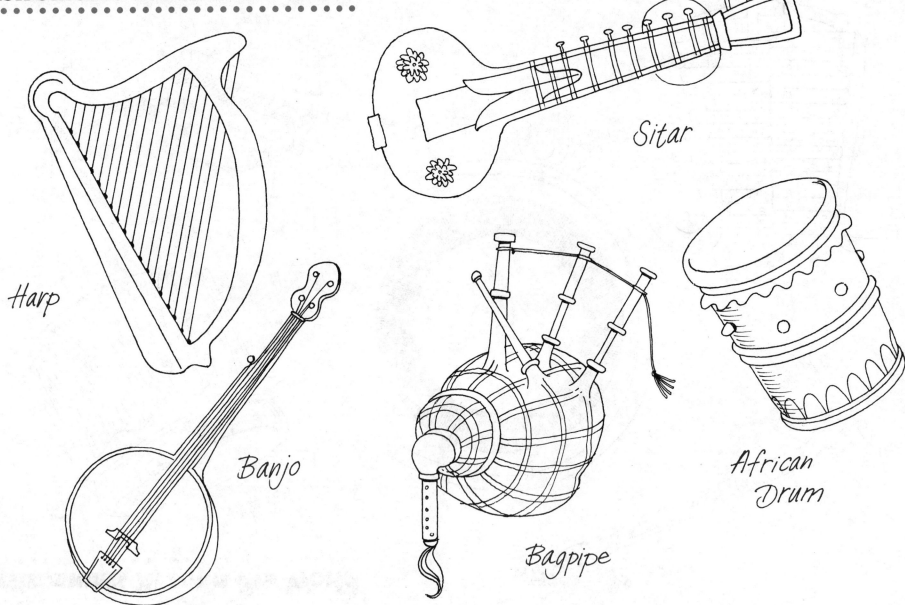

Harp

Sitar

Banjo

Bagpipe

African Drum

History Quilt

Materials:

- 10" x 10" felt squares, various colors
- fabric scraps
- collage materials
- glue
- fabric markers

Directions:

1. Ask the class to think of questions they would like to ask someone who came to America long ago. Then write up a questionnaire based on those thoughts and questions. Make sure to include such questions as:

Who was the first person in your family to immigrate to this country?

What type of transportation(s) did you take to come here?

Did you travel alone or with someone?

Where were you born?

How did you come to be living where you are now?

How are things different today from when you were young?

How many people were in your immediate family?

2. Have students interview parents, aunts and uncles, godparents, or grandparents using the questionnaire. If older relatives are not present, children may choose to interview someone in their neighborhood or in a nearby senior citizen's home.

3. When students return with their surveys, divide them into groups of three or four to share the answers they received. Instruct the groups to choose one item from each member's survey that is unique and then pick one member to tell the class about their group's choices.

4. Next, ask each student to sketch a 10" x 10" design that incorporates information about his or her family's past. For example, they may wish to create designs showing representational symbols or figures from one or more of their nationalities or create scenes from past and present times.

5. Distribute 10" x 10" felt squares, fabric scraps, and other collage materials.

6. Have students use the collage materials to re-create their designs on the felt squares. When the squares are done, attach them by overlapping and gluing the edges of the squares together. Display the quilt in a hallway or invite visitors into the classroom to view it. Ask the class to give the quilt a name.

7. When it is time to take the quilt down, hold a lottery and give the quilt to the student who wins. Or cut apart the squares and allow each student to take home his or her own.

Pen Pals

1. Inform the class that they will have an opportunity to write to a student in another country or another part of their own country. Ask them to brainstorm questions they would like to ask children living in other areas. Encourage them to create questions about physical characteristics, home, school, language, favorite food, activities, daily schedule, clothing, travel, and family.

2. Borrow books from the library that show children from other countries and other parts of the class's own country. Help students research what other lands look like, what languages are spoken there, how the people dress, what they like to eat, what they do for recreation, and so on. Explain that pen pals are an ideal way to learn about life in other cultures.

3. To find out more information about pen pals in the United States and other countries, write to:

Dear Pen Pal
P. O. Box 4054, Dept. UF
Santa Barbara, CA 93103

Once you have the information, distribute it to students and have them get pen pals.

4. Give the class the following tips on writing letters to their pen pals:

Write neatly and clearly, both in the letter and when addressing the envelope.

Tell in the letter whether you are a boy or a girl. Sometimes we have names that are not understood in another country.

Be sure to write your return address on the letter and on the envelope.

Write on such topics as the seasons you experience and the climate where you live.

Write about your favorite holidays and celebrations. Ask about your pen pal's holidays.

Write about a pet or ask about a pet your pen pal may own.

Write about any jobs you have in or outside your homes.

If possible, include a photograph of yourself and ask for one of your pen pal.

5. Ask students to share their pen pal responses with the class when they receive them. Discuss any interesting facts or favorite things the pen pals mention. Create a bulletin board of interesting letters outside the classroom for students in other classes to read.

Happy Birthday to All

Ask the class to share how they celebrate their birthdays. Do they go somewhere special? Do they have a cake? Do they get presents? Do they have their favorite dishes cooked for a birthday dinner? Discuss any differences among the celebrations, and then share the following information with them.

Explain to the class that birthday celebrations came about because long ago, many people believed that a birthday was a time of change from one year to another. Some thought evil spirits came to a person on his or her birthday. To keep the evil spirits away, family and friends surrounded the birthday person so that evil spirits could not get close enough to do harm. The earlier in the day gifts and greetings were given, the better the protection.

In some countries, such as Greece, children usually celebrate name days instead of their birthdays. Children who are named after saints celebrate on the day chosen to honor that saint. They begin their day by going to church and hearing about the life of the saint whose day is being recognized. After

services are over, callers visit throughout the day, bringing gifts. Treats are served to the visitors and family. People who cannot make a visit send cards to the person whose name day it is. Sometimes a special dinner is prepared, or a party may be held.

In Ghana, birthdays were not important days until American and British missionaries began influencing the people. Now, birthdays are very popular. A mother often cooks a special dinner for the birthday child, making all his or her favorite dishes. A mother invites all her child's friends to this dinner, which is eaten in the late afternoon. After dinner, the children all play together. Gifts are not very important; it is the eating and playing together that make the day special.

If desired, ask each child to research how birthdays are celebrated in a different country. After students have completed their research, ask them to share their findings with the class.

My "Me" Book

1. Discuss with the students what they look like, the kinds of clothing they like to wear, and their personalities. Encourage the students to look in a mirror and write down all the adjectives they can to describe themselves. Then have them talk about their clothing. Do they like wearing pants (baggy or tight), dresses, skirts, sneakers or shoes, boots or sandals? Then have each student draw a self-portrait.

2. Help each child make a "Me" book by giving him or her paper, glue, scissors, and a stack of old magazines and workbooks. Ask each child to make a collage of his or her favorite foods. If the student cannot find a picture of something, encourage him or her to draw it, then glue it onto the collage. (If desired, have the class share one or two of their favorite dishes.)

3. Talk about what students like to do on weekends and during their free time on weekdays. Have them write letters to themselves telling about what they like to do, who their favorite people are (sports figures, entertainers, role models), what their hopes for the future are, any problems they may be having, and anything else they wish to write about. Tell them that no one will read the letters. Put each child's letter into an envelope with the child's name on it and seal the envelope.

4. Reproduce the face on page 23 for each student. Have each child color a face and cut it out. Then encourage children to decorate their "faces" with yarn for hair, sparkles for eyes, fabric scraps for hats or hair ornaments, and buttons or beads for earrings or necklaces.

5. Glue each child's "face" to a piece of oaktag to use as the cover for the child's "Me" book. Punch three holes on the left side of each child's envelope, cover, and collage and portrait pages and then bind the "Me" books together with yarn.

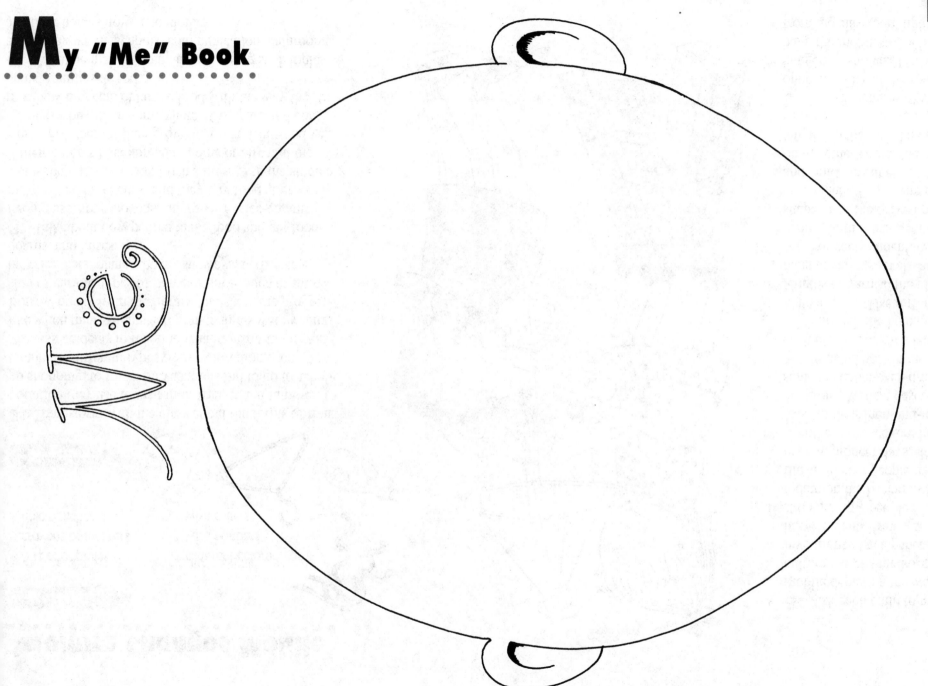

Culture Changes Mobile

Materials:

- 5" paper plates
- crayons or markers
- hole puncher
- different-colored yarns
- wire hangers
- wire cutters

Directions:

1. Brainstorm with the class about the forms of transportation they use to visit their friends and families, to go shopping, to travel on vacation, and to go to school. Graph the different types of transportation used.

2. Ask students to imagine what transportation was like when their parents and grandparents were young. Borrow books from the library that show the progression of various types of transportation, such as trains, bicycles, cars, planes, boats, subways, taxis, skateboards, and buses.

3. Talk about how people make food and get food. People use stoves, ovens, microwaves, ice-cream makers, and barbecues, and they buy food at grocery stores, butcher shops, and fish stores. Ask the students if their parents make bread at home or buy it at the store. Ask them if they grow their own fruits and vegetables or buy them somewhere. Compare and contrast how pioneers obtained food with the way the students' families do today.

4. Continue making comparisons, using such topics as keeping warm, schools, communication, bathrooms, and their homes, toys, and clothes.

5. Ask each child to make a mobile depicting the way our culture has changed because of inventions. On a paper plate, have students draw a scene showing how people get around today; on the back, have them illustrate how people traveled back in pioneer days. Repeat for other areas covered by the class in their then-and-now discussions. Write a descriptive sentence under each drawing.

6. Punch a hole in the top of each plate. Thread a length of yarn through the hole in each plate and tie. Use different lengths of yarn so the plates will hang at various levels, as shown.

7. For each student, twist a hanger until it has a round shape. Cut the curved part of the hanger off with wire cutters, and bend the cut edges in. Then tie the other end of the yarn lengths to the round hanger, as shown.

8. Tie 18" lengths of yarn to opposite sides of the rounded hanger, as shown. Use this to hang the mobiles on a hook or from the classroom lights.

Famous Sites File-Folder Game

Materials:

- crayons or markers
- scissors
- letter-sized file folder
- glue
- oaktag
- clear contact paper
- scraps of different-colored construction paper
- envelope
- die

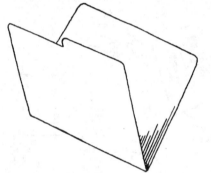

Directions:

1. Reproduce the game board once. Color the game board and cut it out. Glue the board to the inside of a letter-sized file folder.

2. Reproduce the game cards eight times. Color the cards, mount them on oaktag, and cut them out. If desired, laminate them, using clear contact paper.

3. To make playing pieces, cut out shapes resembling small suitcases from the construction paper. Make sure each case is a different color. Mount them on oaktag and laminate them.

4. Reproduce the "How to Play" directions once. Cut out the directions and then glue them to the front of the file folder.

5. Glue an envelope to the back of the file folder to use as storage for game cards and playing pieces.

How to Play (for two to four players)

1. All players place their pieces on "Start." Shuffle all the Wonder Cards and place them facedown next to the game board.

2. The youngest player goes first. Players roll the die and move the number of spaces indicated.

3. If a player lands on a Wonder Card space, he or she takes a card from the pile. If it is a card showing a place not previously collected or paired, the player may keep the card. If it is a card no longer needed because the player already has that pair, the card is placed on the bottom of the game card pile.

4. When a player makes a Wonder Card match, he or she may move directly to the place shown on the card and take another game card.

5. Players continue traveling around the board collecting Wonder Cards. The first player to collect matched pairs of cards for all eight sites is the winner.

Famous Sites File-Folder Game

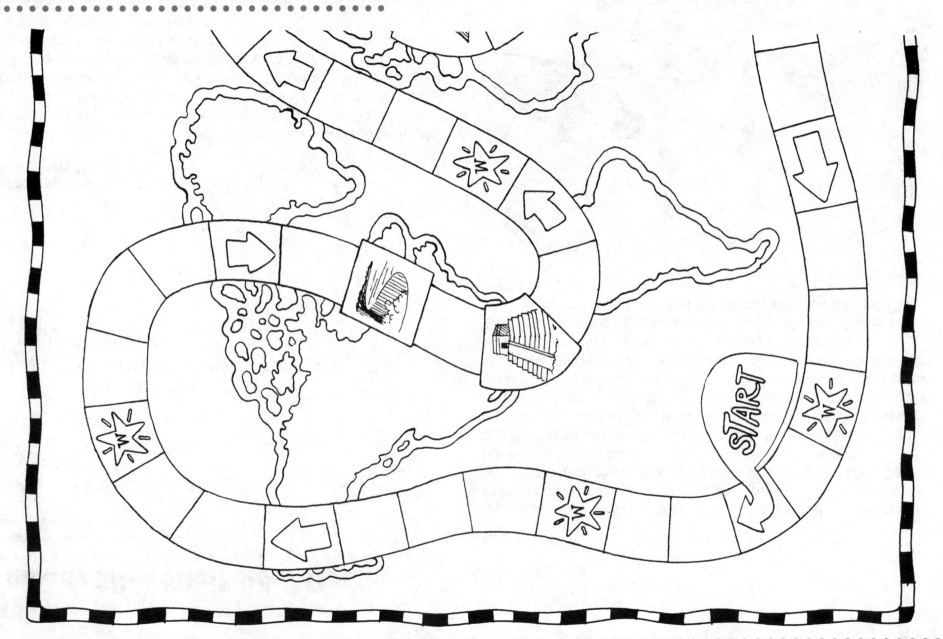

Famous Sites File-Folder Game

Famous Sites File-Folder Game

Taj Mahal

Niagara Falls

Sphinx

Mayan Ruins

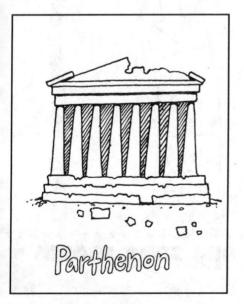

Parthenon

Eiffel Tower

Kremlin

Great Wall

Best Stories from Around the World

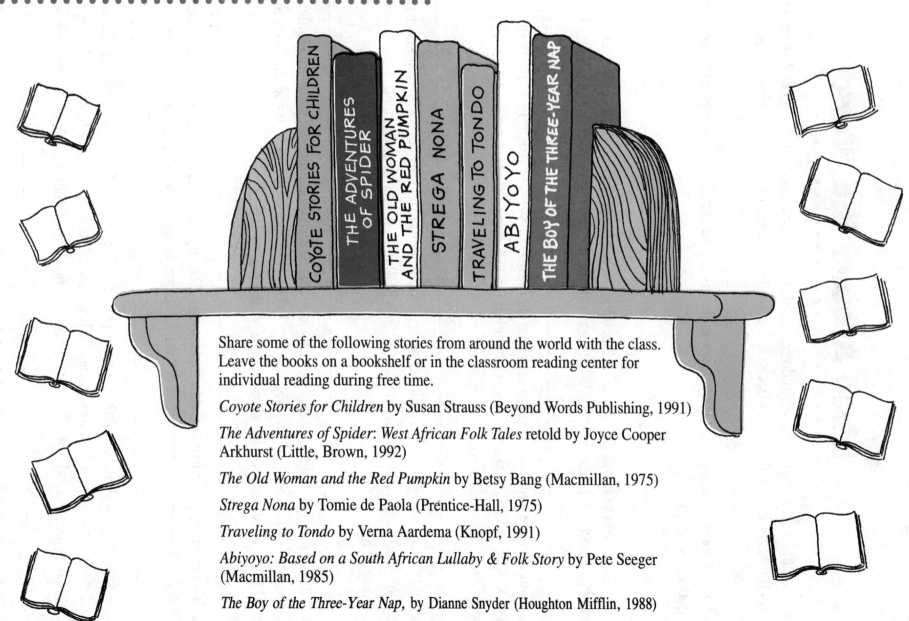

Share some of the following stories from around the world with the class. Leave the books on a bookshelf or in the classroom reading center for individual reading during free time.

Coyote Stories for Children by Susan Strauss (Beyond Words Publishing, 1991)

The Adventures of Spider: West African Folk Tales retold by Joyce Cooper Arkhurst (Little, Brown, 1992)

The Old Woman and the Red Pumpkin by Betsy Bang (Macmillan, 1975)

Strega Nona by Tomie de Paola (Prentice-Hall, 1975)

Traveling to Tondo by Verna Aardema (Knopf, 1991)

Abiyoyo: Based on a South African Lullaby & Folk Story by Pete Seeger (Macmillan, 1985)

The Boy of the Three-Year Nap, by Dianne Snyder (Houghton Mifflin, 1988)

Time Around the World

Clocks in different parts of the world do not all show the same time. If it is 3:00 P.M. in New York, it is 8:00 P.M. in England. This is because the world is divided into 24 *time zones*, based on the earth's rotation around the sun.

Look in a telephone book or an encyclopedia for an international time zone chart. Then answer the questions below.

1. At 2:00 P.M., you win first prize in a spelling contest in New York. You can't wait to call your friend in Ireland to tell her about it. What time will the phone ring in your friend's house in Ireland?

_____

2. Your favorite aunt is coming to visit from her home in Sydney, Australia. Her flight leaves at 10:00 A.M. and will take two hours to land in Hong Kong. What time will she arrive in Hong Kong?

_____

3. Your father told you not to call him after 11:00 P.M. in Cairo, Egypt. But your sister just had a baby and you want to tell him immediately! It's 8:30 P.M. in London, England, where you live. Can you call him?

_____

4. Your family is taking a car trip from Vancouver, British Columbia, Canada, to Seattle, Washington, United States. The trip is going to last five hours. If you arrive at the hotel in Seattle at 2:00 P.M., what time did the family leave Vancouver?

_____

5. It's your first plane trip to Orlando, Florida. The flight is scheduled to arrive in Orlando at 7:00 A.M. The flight takes four hours from Chicago, Illinois. What time did you leave Chicago?

_____

6. A note on your desk says that you got a phone call at 5:00 P.M. from a cousin in Mexico City, Mexico. You live in San Antonio, Texas. When you call him back a half hour later, he says he has been waiting for your call for more than 1 hour. Is he right? If not, how long has he been waiting?

_____

People Habitats Dioramas

Materials:

- shoe boxes
- crayons and markers
- different types of paper (construction, foil, tissue)
- scissors
- collage materials
- glue
- tape
- thread

Directions:

1. Discuss with the class the types of habitats in which people live, such as the country, the city, the mountains, the plains, and the beach. What types of houses do you think people need to blend in with their various environments? For example, people who live underground need some way to get light and air and water into their houses. They need houses that do not let in the rain or the cold.

2. Ask the class to think of a place, imaginary or real, and create a home for people who live in this place. Invite the class to choose a shoe box to be the structure for their environment. Provide students with plenty of crayons and markers, construction paper, foil, tissue paper, collage materials, and glue.

3. When they have decided what their backgrounds will look like, have students decorate the insides of their shoe box dioramas to resemble their imagined places. They may also wish to decorate the outsides in keeping with the environment of the insides.

4. Each student may then make a house that would blend in with the chosen surroundings. The house may be underground, under the sea, suspended in the air (from the top of the box using thread), or on the ground. Lastly, make the people who could live in the house and the environment. Will they have any special physical features that have been adapted to their environment? Do they need special clothing to survive there? Can they have pets? What types of animals could be their pets?

5. Make a gallery of dioramas and encourage the class to walk around looking at the different "people habitats." Compare and contrast the different ways students presented similar environments.

Fairy Tales Around the World

Explain to the class that many countries have their own versions of popular fairy tales. After reading the Grimm Brothers' version of "Cinderella" to the class, share these other versions of "Cinderella":

Perrault's Fairy Tales ("Cinderella, or The Little Glass Slipper") translated by Sasha Moorsom (Doubleday, 1972)

Princess Furball retold by Charlotte Huck (Greenwillow, 1989)

Mufaro's Beautiful Daughters by John Steptoe (Lothrop, Lee, 1987)

Cinderella
by the Brothers Grimm

There once was a rich man who had a wife and a young daughter. One day, the wife became very sick. She called her daughter to her bed and told her to always be good and kind. "I promise, Mother," the daughter said. A few days later, the woman died.

One year later, the man married again. His new wife and her two daughters came to live in the house. The new wife and her daughters did not like the man's daughter. They took away her pretty clothes and gave her an old ugly dress to wear. They made her eat alone in the kitchen instead of the dining room. They forced her to clean the house, carry water, light the fire, cook, and do laundry. They even called her Cinderella because she was always so dirty from the ashes and cinders from the fireplace.

But no matter how mean her stepsisters and stepmother were to her, Cinderella remembered her promise to her own mother, and was always good and kind.

Cinderella was also very sad. She would visit her mother's grave every day. One day, her father was going into town and asked the girls what they would like him to bring them. Both stepsisters asked for beautiful dresses and jewels. Cinderella just asked for the first twig that might brush his hat on his way home. When he returned, he gave his stepdaughters their clothes and jewels, and he gave Cinderella the twig from a hazel tree that had caught on his hat.

She brought the twig to her mother's grave. Cinderella planted it over her grave and cried so much that the twig grew roots and began to grow. Every time she visited her mother's grave after that, a white bird would sit in the tree and listen to Cinderella's wishes. The bird would throw down whatever she wished for.

Then, one day, the King proclaimed a three-day festival to find a bride for his son, the Prince. Cinderella wanted to go, but her stepmother and stepsisters laughed at her. They called her names and pointed out how dirty she was. But Cinderella begged her stepmother so much that the stepmother said she could go—if she could pick out all the lentils from the fire ashes within two hours.

Cinderella brought a bucket to the window and called for all her bird friends to help her. They finished within one hour. When Cinderella brought the bucket of ashes and the bowl of clean lentils for her stepmother to see, the stepmother told Cinderella she still could not go. The stepmother said Cinderella would only embarrass them because she was so dirty.

Fairy Tales Around the World

Cinderella went out to the hazel tree and asked the white bird for clothes to wear to the festival. On the grave appeared a beautiful gold and silver gown and a pair of matching slippers. She went to the festival, and no one knew who she was. When the Prince saw her, he danced with no one else. When it was time for Cinderella to go home, she slipped away into the night.

The next night, Cinderella asked the white bird again for clothes to wear to the festival. Again no one recognized her, again the Prince danced only with her, and again she left without him finding out who she was or where she lived.

On the last night, the bird threw down the most magnificent gown anyone had ever seen, along with a pair of slippers made of pure gold. Later, when Cinderella wanted to leave, the Prince had already worked out a plan to find out who she was. He had the steps waxed so that when Cinderella ran out, one of her slippers got stuck in the sticky wax.

The Prince went house to house the next day to find who could fit into the shoe. When it was her turn, the first stepdaughter took the shoe and put it on. Her foot was too long. The stepmother told her to cut off her toes and she did. When the shoe fit, the Prince rode off with his new bride. But as they passed Cinderella's hazel tree, two white doves sitting in the tree told the Prince to look down at the trail of blood and to go back to the house for the true bride. The Prince saw all the blood and went back to the house.

The second stepdaughter tried on the shoe, but her heel stuck out. The stepmother told her to cut off her heel, and she did. When the shoe fit, the Prince rode off with his new bride. But as they passed Cinderella's hazel tree, the white doves told the Prince to look down at the trail of blood and to go back to the house for the true bride.

When the Prince came back, the father told the Prince there was only his unkempt daughter from his first wife left in the house. But the Prince made Cinderella try on the shoe anyway and when it fit, he rode off with her. As they passed the hazel tree, the two white doves flew down and sat on her shoulders. On the day of the wedding, Cinderella's two stepsisters stood on either side of her. On the way to the wedding, the white doves pecked out one eye from each sister. On the way back from the wedding, the white doves pecked out the other eye from each sister. The doves had punished them with blindness for the rest of their lives for all their wickedness. And Cinderella and the prince lived happily ever after.

Ask the class some discussion questions after they have read the different versions of this story, such as:

1. How was the main character in each version different or similar?

2. When Cinderella wanted consolation, what did she do in each version?

3. Who helped Cinderella go to the festival ball?

4. Why did Cinderella leave the ball in each version?

5. How were the outcomes different or similar in each version?

Cinderella Flannel Board

Reproduce the story characters on this page and page 35. Color the figures and cut them out. Then glue flannel scraps to the back of each figure. Add the figures to the flannel board as the characters appear in the story. Later, let children use the figures to recreate the story or to make up their own.

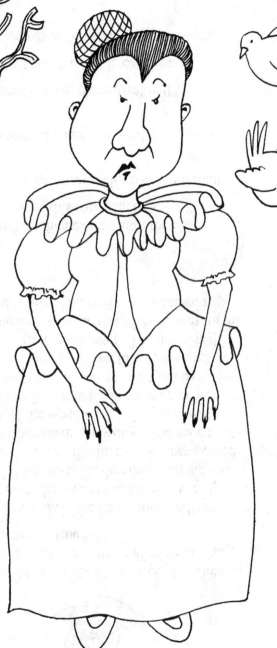

Cinderella Flannel Board

Native American Friends

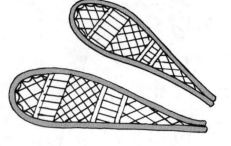

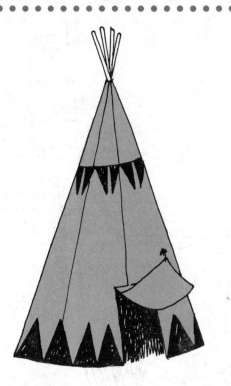

Have a class discussion about Native Americans. Explain that there are many different American Indian groups in North and South America. Each group, or tribe, has its own special customs, language, clothing styles, food, and religious beliefs. While many of these things are similar from group to group, each Indian tribe is unique.

Talk about the way Native Americans lived long ago, and the way they live today. Explain that in modern times American Indians live all over; some live in towns and cities, and some live on reservations, which are tracts of land set aside by the federal government for Native Americans.

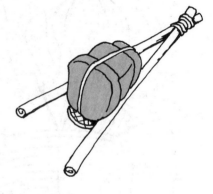

Ask if anyone can name the types of homes Native Americans lived in. Tell the class that some homes, such as the Navajo hogan and the Hopi pueblo, are still used today. Other homes, such as the Sioux tipi, the Iroquois longhouse, and the Seminole chickee, are no longer used. The type of shelter depended on the climate in which each tribe lived. Encourage children to research the different kinds of dwellings and draw pictures of their favorite ones. Or help the class construct a mural depicting Native American dwellings, using paint and collage materials.

You may also wish to talk about the types of transportation used by Native Americans, such as dugout canoes, travois (see illustration), snowshoes, and horses. If desired, ask children to research these methods of transportation and draw pictures or add to their mural.

An important point to make to young children is that Native Americans have often been portrayed in stereotypical ways in books, songs, television shows, and films. Stress that some depictions of American Indians are unfair and prejudiced. Emphasize the varied, rich culture and history of Native Americans instead.

Native American Sand Painting

Materials:

- pencils
- cardboard or oaktag
- colored sand
- glue

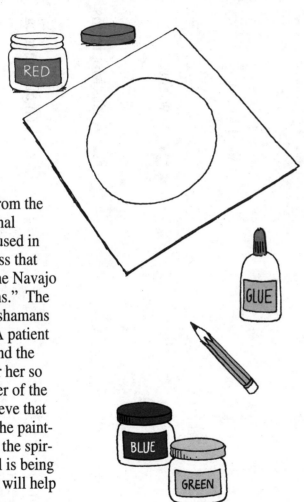

Directions:

1. Borrow some books from the library to research traditional Native American designs used in sand painting. Tell the class that sand painting is done by the Navajo medicine men, or "shamans." The designs are created as the shamans chant ceremonial songs. A patient sits in the sand painting, and the sand is rubbed over him or her so he or she absorbs the power of the painting. The Navajo believe that as the shaman is creating the paint- ing and chanting his song, the spir- its will come to see that all is being done correctly. If so, they will help to heal the patient.

2. Have students create sand paintings of their own. Tell each child to begin by drawing a design on a piece of cardboard or sturdy oaktag.

3. Squeeze some glue onto one section of the design at a time, spreading it over the section with a finger. Then gently pour the desired color sand over the glued section. Turn the cardboard to the side and tap it until all the excess sand comes off. Then begin the next section in the same way.

4. Share books with the class that feature artistic expressions from other cultures. Although artists from many different cultures use the same media to create their art, they often use unique materials or have a unique way of presenting their work that reflects their culture. Compare and contrast media and materials of different cultures.

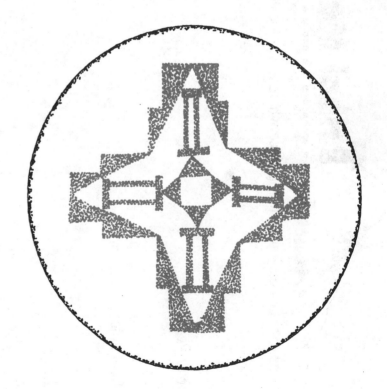

Name _____

Tribal Match

Draw a line to match each tribe to the place where it was located.

1. Nez Percé

2. Seminole

3. Iroquois

4. Sioux

5. Kwakuitl

6. Aztec

7. Inca

8. Navajo

9. Algonquian

10. Omaha

a. North Dakota, South Dakota

b. California

c. Arizona

d. Nebraska

e. Oregon

f. Florida

g. New York

h. Andes Mountains

i. Central America

j. Ontario, Canada

Naturally Colorful

Materials:

- vegetables, fruits, berries
- knife
- wooden spoon
- strainer
- small bowls
- wool yarn or cloth
- salt
- vinegar

Directions:

1. Tell students that Native Americans used vibrant colors to decorate their homes, clothing, toys, tools, and many other objects. They made these dyes and paints from things found in nature.

2. To make natural dyes, cut a colored vegetable, fruit, or berry into small pieces.

3. Mash the food in a strainer. Place a small bowl under the strainer to catch the juices. Then rub strands of wool yarn or cloth in the bowl until they become dyed.

4. Use several different kinds of food to make different colors of dye. For example, you may wish to use spinach for a green dye (first boil the spinach, then drain the water), or raspberries for a red dye.

5. To make natural paints, mix approximately 1 cup of colored berries with 1 teaspoon of salt and 1 teaspoon of vinegar. Let children dip their paintbrushes into each color and paint pictures. (An option for red paint is to dissolve red clay into water.)

Name _____

Poetry in Nature

Many Native American poems and folktales are about nature. Through these stories, Native Americans often showed their appreciation of the beauty of nature or tried to explain something that occurs in nature, such as thunder and lightning or the habits of a particular animal.

Read the poem below. On a separate piece of paper, write a poem or a folktale about something in nature. Then draw a picture to go with your story!

May I Walk
(Navajo)

On the trail marked with pollen may I walk,

With grasshoppers about my feet may I walk,

With dew about my feet may I walk,

With beauty may I walk,

With beauty before me, may I walk,

With beauty behind me, may I walk,

With beauty above me, may I walk,

With beauty under me, may I walk,

With beauty all around me, may I walk,

In old age wandering on a trail of beauty, lively, may I walk,

In old age wandering on a trail of beauty, living again, may I walk,

It is finished in beauty.

People of Africa

Ask the class if anyone can locate the continent of Africa on a world map. Explain to children that Africa is a large continent made up of many different countries and cultures. Africa today has modern cities and towns as well as traditional villages.

Emphasize the varied, rich culture and history of Africa. Discuss the fact that the ancestors of African Americans originally lived in Africa. Most of these people were brought to America against their will on slave ships long ago. Many modern-day African American families try to use African customs and values in their own homes as a way of preserving their culture and history. One important holiday that emphasizes African culture is Kwanzaa, which is celebrated from December 26 to January 1.

Ask if any volunteers can name the types of homes Africans lived in historically and today. Grass and mud houses with thatched roofs may still be seen in Chad and other western countries, and houses along the western coast are still built on stilts.

Most Africans today, however, live in modern houses. Encourage children to research the different types of dwellings and draw pictures of their favorite ones. Or help the class construct a mural depicting African dwellings, using paint and collage materials.

You may also wish to talk about the kinds of clothing worn in Africa. If possible, show children examples of Kente cloth, which has vibrant colors and patterns, or Ashanti cloth, which has painted patterns. Try to find books that show traditional types of dress, such as the gele, a scarf that is wrapped around a woman's head like a turban, and the dashiki, a ceremonial tunic that is worn by Nigerian men.

If possible, show examples of African jewelry, masks, shields, and other unique art. Make the "African beads" described on page 44, and discuss the works of influential African and African American artists. Can students see traditional African designs in these works?

Name _____

Swahili Word Search

Find the Swahili words from the box below that are hidden in this puzzle. The words may appear forward, backward, up, down, or diagonally.

```
C  J  O  T  O  T  A  W
G  H  T  E  M  B  O  K
S  W  A  H  I  L  I  A
K  G  I  K  I  F  A  R
B  A  B  A  U  J  G  I
O  B  M  A  J  L  K  B
J  A  N  G  O  M  A  U
M  L  A  H  A  W  S  K
```

Swahili—language spoken in many parts of Africa	**rafiki—friend**
	karibu—welcome
	jambo—hello
mama—mother	**chakula—food**
baba—father	**tembo—elephant**
watoto—children	**ngoma—drum**

African Foods

Sample these foods with the class during study units about Africa.

Fried Bananas
(serves approximately 12 to 15 students)

Materials:

- 6 medium or large bananas
- plastic knives
- lemon juice
- brown sugar
- cinnamon
- butter
- frying pan
- spatula
- paper towels

Directions:

1. Ask several children to peel and cut six bananas into 1/2" slices.

2. Place the banana slices on a large plate. Sprinkle a little lemon juice, brown sugar, and cinnamon onto the slices.

3. Put some butter in a frying pan over medium heat. Place a layer of banana slices in the frying pan.

4. Fry both sides of the banana slices until golden. Drain on paper towels and then serve.

Chocolate Heaven

Tell students that cocoa and chocolate are made from the beans of cacao trees, which are found in the tropical rain forests of Africa. Ask students to name some different kinds of chocolate and ways in which chocolate and cocoa are used. If possible, let children sample several types of chocolate and describe the differences in taste.

Help the class prepare old-fashioned hot chocolate on a cold winter's day. Mix together 1/3 cup of cocoa, 1 cup of sugar, and 3 quarts of milk in a saucepan over medium heat. (Serves approximately 15 students.) Enjoy!

African Beads

Materials:

- saucepan
- 2 cups cornstarch
- 5 cups baking soda
- wooden spoon
- large mixing bowl
- embroidery needle
- paint and paintbrushes
- dental floss

Directions:

1. To make beads to use in creating bracelets and necklaces, begin by placing 3 1/2 cups of cold water in a saucepan over medium heat. Then add in 2 cups of cornstarch and 5 cups of baking soda.

2. Stir continuously until the mixture becomes thick and claylike.

3. Remove the clay from the heat and place in a large mixing bowl.

4. When the clay has cooled enough to touch, let each child take a small portion. Show students how to make small balls with the clay.

5. Help each student poke an embroidery needle through each ball of clay. Provide children with paint and paintbrushes to use to decorate these beads.

6. Show children how to thread dental floss through the balls. Students may string together as many beads as they wish to make bracelets or necklaces for themselves or to give as gifts for Kwanzaa and other holidays.

African Folk Tale

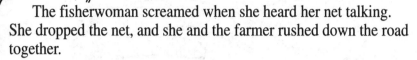

"Talk"

Long ago, there lived a man who wanted to dig up some yams from his garden. As soon as he started to dig, one of the yams called out, "Stop that! You never took the time to give me any water, and now you're poking me. Just go away!"

The man was quite startled. He looked at his dog, who was standing nearby. "Did you just say something?" he asked the dog, who had never before spoken a word.

"No," said the dog. "It was the yam talking. He wants you to go away."

The man began to get a little frightened. He went over to a big tree to break off a branch so he could hit the dog. "Hey!" shouted the tree. "Who do you think you are, breaking a branch off me!"

Now the man was really frightened. He threw the branch down on the ground. "Don't throw me down so hard!" complained the branch. "Put me down gently!"

"Get that branch off me!" added the stone on which the branch had landed.

The man rushed away, stumbling in terror. Before too long, he came upon a fisherwoman.

"What's your hurry?" said the fisherwoman.

"My yam said, 'Go away!' and my dog told me to listen to the yam. Then the tree shouted at me for breaking off a branch, and the branch yelled at me for throwing him down too hard. Finally, the stone said, 'Get that branch off me!'" the man said breathlessly.

"What is so frightening about all that?" said the fisherwoman.

"Yes," said the net she was carrying. "That doesn't sound very scary at all."

The fisherwoman screamed when she heard her net talking. She dropped the net, and she and the farmer rushed down the road together.

Soon they came upon a seamstress with a large bundle of cloth in her arms. "Why are you running so madly?" she asked.

The farmer and the fisherwoman explained what had happened.

"Why, that's no reason to be worried," the seamstress said.

"Sure, it is," said the bundle of cloth. "No doubt you would be worried if it happened to you."

The seamstress screamed and flung the bundle of cloth. Then she ran down the road with the farmer and the fisherwoman.

Next the group came to a child swimming in the river. They told him what had happened.

"Is that why you are all running so foolishly?" he asked.

"I think you might run just as foolishly," the river retorted.

The frightened child scrambled up the river bank and ran down the road with the group. Finally, they came to the house of the village chief. The chief listened carefully to their incredible story. Then he spoke.

"I must scold you all for telling such wild tales," he said sternly. "You have gotten the whole village in a panic with your nonsense. Now, go back and stop telling such lies."

The four people left in shame. As the chief sat down on his favorite stool he said to himself, "Some people have the craziest thoughts."

"I couldn't agree with you more," said the stool. "After all, who has ever heard of a talking yam?"

"Talk" Stick Puppets

Reproduce the figures on this page and on pages 47 and 48 once. Color the figures, mount them on oaktag, and cut them out. Then glue a craft stick to the back of each figure. Use the stick puppets when reading the folk tale "Talk." Leave the puppets out for students to use for dramatic play during free time.

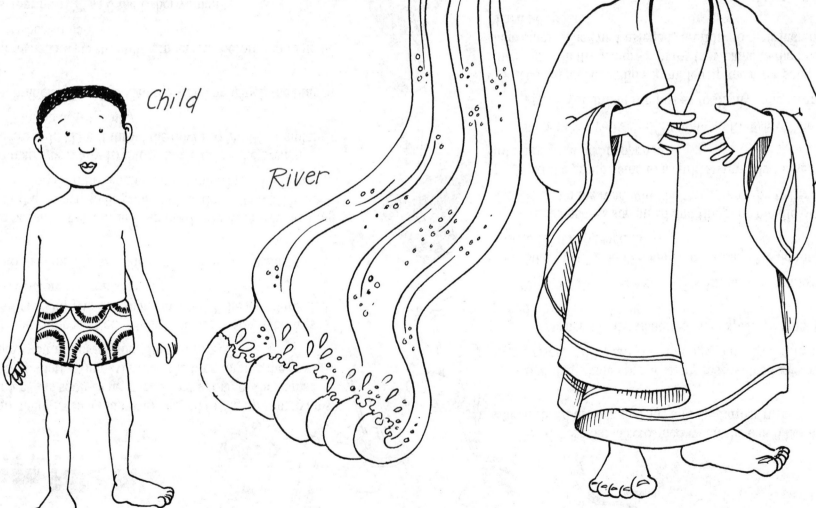

Child

River

Man

"Talk" Stick Puppets

Fisher-woman

Chief

Seamstress

"Talk" Stick Puppets

Branch

Yam

Dog

Net

Tree

Stone

Bundle

Spanish Bingo

- markers
- 8 1/2" x 11" white paper
- glue
- oaktag
- scissors
- construction paper

Directions:

1. Draw a four-square by four-square, or a five-square by five-square, bingo board on an 8 1/2" x 11" piece of white paper. Copy the paper once for each child.

2. Have children mount the boards on oaktag and cut them out.

3. Collect the boards. Write a different numeral from 1 to 10 (or 1 to 20) randomly in each square of a board. Repeat for the other boards, making sure that no two boards are alike.

4. Distribute construction paper scraps to the class. Ask students to cut out enough circles to cover each number on their game boards.

5. Play the game of "Bingo" by calling out the Spanish word for each number (e.g., "uno" for "one"). Decide before each game what figure on the bingo board will win, such as one row, a picture frame, the letter *T*, or the entire board. Have children use the construction paper circles to cover any numbers that are called.

6. Variations of this game may be played with addition and subtraction facts or simple Spanish vocabulary words.

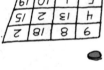

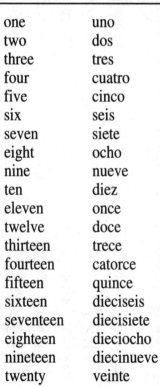

one	uno
two	dos
three	tres
four	cuatro
five	cinco
six	seis
seven	siete
eight	ocho
nine	nueve
ten	diez
eleven	once
twelve	doce
thirteen	trece
fourteen	catorce
fifteen	quince
sixteen	dieciseis
seventeen	diecisiete
eighteen	dieciocho
nineteen	diecinueve
twenty	veinte

Mexican Crossword

Fill in the Spanish word for each English word below to complete the crossword.

Across

1. party
4. clay bricks
7. good morning
8. thank you
12. book
13. female friend
14. large
15. family

Down

2. good-bye
3. hat
5. hello
6. yes
9. house

10. male friend
11. green
13. blue

Excellent Enchiladas

Materials:

- frying pan
- tortillas
- vegetable oil
- paper towels
- grater
- cheddar cheese
- onions
- large baking pan
- enchilada sauce

4. Help students roll their tortillas. Put the tortillas in a large baking pan.

5. Spoon enchilada sauce over the tops of the tortillas. Bake at 375° for approximately 15 minutes.

6. If desired, take students on a field trip to a local Mexican restaurant. Help children prepare questions for the owner or chef about the different types of food used, how special dishes are prepared, what the restaurant's specialty is, and so on.

Directions:

1. Fry each tortilla in vegetable oil until golden brown. Remove from heat and place on a paper towel to drain.

2. Ask one group of children to grate some cheddar cheese. Help another group of children dice some onions.

3. When the tortillas are cool enough to touch, let each child place some cheese and onions in the center of a tortilla, as shown.

Mexican Birthday Song

Celebrate a group of class birthdays by teaching students the following song. If desired, help children learn how to do a simple version of the Mexican Hat Dance, which is often performed at birthday parties, by following the directions below.

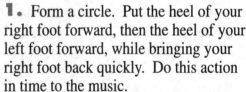

1. Form a circle. Put the heel of your right foot forward, then the heel of your left foot forward, while bringing your right foot back quickly. Do this action in time to the music.

2. Circle to the right, then to the left. Then join hands and move to the center of the circle while raising hands high in the air.

3. Dance back to the original circle position, bending at the waist. Repeat.

Las Mañanitas

Estas son las mañanitas
Que cantaba el rey David.
A las muchachas bonitas
Se les cantaba así:
Despierta, mi bien, despierta,
Mira que ya amaneció
Y los pajaritos cantan
La luna ya se metió.

You may also wish to show students how to make tissue-paper flowers to decorate the classroom for a party. Simply place four 6" x 6" squares of different-colored tissue paper together. Gather together in the middle, as shown, and bind with a pipe cleaner that will come down as the stem.

My Own Poncho

© 1996 Troll Early Learning Activities

Materials:

- 18" x 30" colored felt or burlap
- scissors
- plastic needles
- colored yarn
- permanent markers, puff paints (optional)

Directions:

1. Give each child an 18" x 30" piece of colored felt or burlap. Help each student cut a hole in the center of the fabric large enough for his or her head to fit through.

2. Show children how to use scissors to fringe the bottoms of their ponchos.

3. Have children sketch out designs for their ponchos on blank paper. Then help each child use a large plastic needle and various colors of yarn to transfer these designs onto his or her poncho.

4. If desired, students may also use permanent markers or puff paints to decorate their ponchos.

5. Tell students that ponchos are worn by men, women, and children in Mexico and other countries where people from Spain once settled. Ask volunteers to tell what they like about wearing ponchos.

Chinese Culture

When introducing a study unit about China and its people, emphasize the rich history and culture of the Chinese people. Tell students that China's history extends back more than 5,000 years, and that its contributions to other cultures and to world history are immeasurable.

Ask if anyone can describe a traditional Chinese home. Explain that most homes in the past were made up of just one room. Homes were usually built from red brick. Families often lived in clusters around a central courtyard, where much of their free time was spent. Today, many Chinese people live in modern apartment buildings or in single-family homes that are larger than the traditional homes.

The bicycle is the most popular form of transportation in China. People use bicycles to get to work, school, friends' homes, the market, and just about everywhere else. If possible, find a picture of a Chinese urban area showing the large number of cyclists on the road. Explain to students that very few Chinese families own other vehicles, and that automobiles are not used nearly as frequently as they are in the United States, Canada, and many other countries.

Tell students that Chinese children learn calligraphy from a very young age. Show the class several examples of calligraphy, in English and in Chinese. If desired, provide children with pens and black ink and let them try to imitate this type of writing.

Chinese children also enjoy playing many different games, such as shuttle-cock (badminton), jump rope, and tug of war.

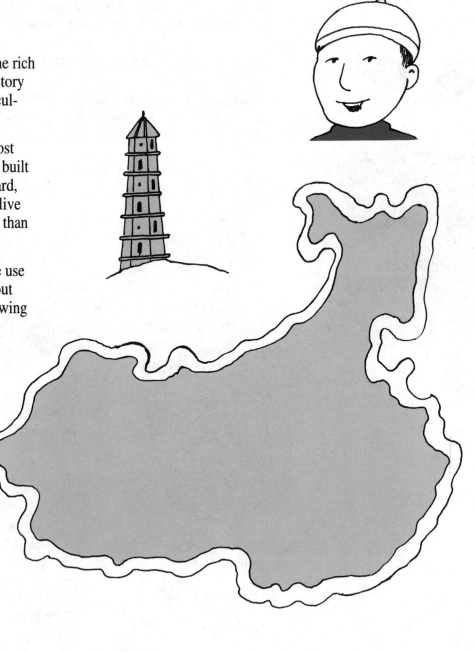

Panda Face Mask

- crayons or markers
- glue
- oaktag
- scissors
- hole puncher
- 12" lengths of yarn

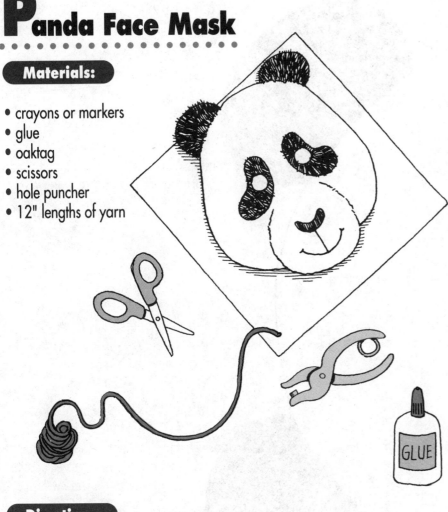

1. Reproduce the mask on page 56 once for each child. Have students color the masks, mount them on oaktag, and cut them out.

2. Help each child cut out the eye holes for the mask.

3. Punch a hole on either side of the mask where indicated.

4. Tie a 12" length of yarn to each hole. Then tie to fit around each child's head.

5. Review these fun panda facts with students.

- There are two kinds of pandas: the giant panda and the red panda. The giant panda is a large animal with black-and-white coloring. The red panda is much smaller and reddish-brown in color.
- Adult pandas weigh up to 350 pounds.
- When panda cubs are born, they only weigh a few ounces.
- Pandas eat bamboo shoots, along with some other plants.
- Pandas live in bamboo forests in the mountains of China.

Panda Face Mask

Name _____

Chinese Numbers

Look at each of the Chinese numbers below. On the lines provided, practice writing the numbers.

一　　**1**　　i ("yee") _____

二　　**2**　　uhr ("er") _____

三　　**3**　　sahn ("sahn") _____

四　　**4**　　suh ("suh") _____

五　　**5**　　wu ("woo") _____

六　　**6**　　liu ("leo") _____

七　　**7**　　chi ("chee") _____

八　　**8**　　ba ("bah") _____

九　　**9**　　ju ("jeo") _____

十　　**10**　　shur ("shur") _____

Cooling Off

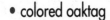

Materials:

- colored oaktag
- scissors
- paints or watercolors and paintbrushes
- crayons or markers
- tissue paper
- decorating materials
- glue
- craft sticks

Directions:

1. Explain to students that in China and Japan, as well as in other Asian countries, beautiful fans are made and used. If possible, show children some hand-painted fans from these countries. Then let children make their own fans, following the steps below.

2. Distribute various colors of oaktag to students. Ask each child to cut out a simple shape about 10" to 12" in diameter.

3. Provide students with paints or watercolors, crayons or markers, stickers, tissue paper, and other decorating materials to use to make their fans.

4. When each child is satisfied with his or her fan, glue a craft stick to the bottom, as shown.

5. Children may wish to use their fans on warm days or give them as gifts to friends or family members for Chinese New Year (celebrated on a different date between January 21 and February 19 each year).

Going to Market

Help explain how shopping for food and other goods varies all over the world by having the class set up a Japanese market one afternoon. Tell children that this is called ichiba, a group of different stores clustered together. People buy fresh produce, meat, fish, and other foods, as well as clothing, shoes, household goods, and other nonfood items.

Ask students to work in groups of two or three children each. Let each group decide what kind of store to run. Go over the list before children actually begin work to make sure different areas have been covered.

Give each group an area (a table, cardboard box, etc.) to use for their store. Have children use items available in the classroom, such as plastic food, paper towels, pencils, and so on, as their stores' merchandise. Encourage students to draw pictures of items they wish to sell as well. Tell children to write prices out for the different items in their stores.

Provide each group with a set amount of play money to use to make purchases at other stores. Let groups take turns "shopping" at the various stores in the ichiba throughout the afternoon.

Go Fly a Kite!

Materials:

- sturdy oaktag or strong nylon fabric
- scissors
- fabric marker
- paints, fabric paints, and paintbrushes
- crayons or markers
- glue

- hole puncher
- dowels
- yarn
- kite string
- fabric strips

Directions:

1. Have each child cut out a kite from sturdy oaktag or strong nylon fabric. Students may cut out any shape or figure they wish, or you may choose to have everyone make a uniform shape, such as an 18" x 18" diamond.

2. Reproduce the stencil patterns on page 61 once for each child. Have children cut out the patterns as indicated.

3. Show students how to trace the stencil patterns onto their kites as they wish, using a pencil or fabric marker.

4. Provide children with paints, fabric paints, and crayons or markers to use to color in their stencils.

5. Punch a hole at the top, right, and bottom of each kite.

6. To make a frame for the kite, glue two dowels of the length and width of the kite together in a "t" shape.

7. Tie a length of yarn to each hole. Then tie the dowel in place with the yarn. Use another length of yarn to strengthen the middle point of the dowel.

8. Attach a piece of kite string (approximately 18" long) to the bottom hole and tie.

9. Tie a roll of kite string to the middle point of the dowels. To complete the kite, add a tail to the bottom, using fabric strips (approximately 12" long).

Kite Stencils

Haikus for Sadako

Read the book *Sadako and the Thousand Paper Cranes* by Eleanor Coerr (Dell, 1977) to the class. Use the story to begin a discussion about cultural differences between where the class lives and Japan. Then ask if anyone knows what a haiku is. Explain to children that a haiku is a type of traditional Japanese poetry that consists of three lines. The first line has five syllables, the second line has seven syllables, and the third line has five syllables. For example:

> Our wonderful world
> The kind breezes gently blow
> All over the land.

Ask each child to write a haiku about something from *Sadako and the Thousand Paper Cranes*. Children may choose to write about school, athletic events, illness, family, or friends. When each student has finished his or her haiku, ask volunteers to share their poems with the class. Then attach the haikus to a wall or a bulletin board under the title "Haikus for Sadako."

Name _____

Everyday Japanese Words

Many words that are used in everyday English are actually Japanese. See how many of the words below you know. Write the definition for each word on the line provided.

1. kimono _____

_____

2. futon _____

_____

3. sayonara _____

_____

4. haiku _____

_____

5. origami _____

6. bonsai _____

_____

7. tofu _____

_____

8. sushi _____

_____

Now practice saying these Japanese words.

Answers

page 5

Answers will vary.

page 15

doll = $5.00	roller skates = $10.00
soccer ball = .50¢	stuffed animal = $3.00
drum = $2.50	sled = $4.00
marbles = $2.00	ball & cup = .25¢

page 30

1. 7:00 P.M
2. 10:00 A.M.
3. yes—it's 10:30 P.M. in Cairo
4. 9:00 A.M.
5. 2:00 A.M.
6. no—he has been waiting 1/2 hour

page 38

1. Nez Percé
2. Seminole
3. Iroquois
4. Sioux
5. Kwakuitl
6. Aztec
7. Inca
8. Navajo
9. Algonquian
10. Omaha

a. North Dakota, South Dakota
b. California
c. Arizona
d. Nebraska
e. Oregon
f. Florida
g. New York
h. Andes Mountains
i. Central America
j. Ontario, Canada

page 42

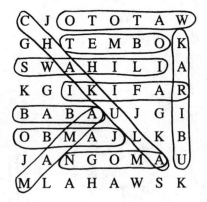

page 50

					¹F	I	E	S	T	³A		
	⁴S									D		
⁵A	D	O	B	E						I		
	M				⁶H		⁷S			O		
⁸B	U	E	N	O	S	D	I	A	S			
	R				L		A					
	E		⁹G	R	A	¹⁰C	I	A	S		¹¹V	
¹²L	I	B	R	O		A		M			E	
	O					S		I			R	
			¹³A	M	I	G	A		¹⁴G	R	A	N	D	E
			Z			O			O		E	
¹⁵F	A	M	I	L	I	A						

page 63

1. kimono—a long, loose robe that is tied at the waist with a sash
2. futon—a thin mattress that can be folded up and used as a couch or chair
3. sayonara—a way to say "good-bye"
4. haiku—an unrhymed poem with 5 syllables in the first line, 7 syllables in the second line, and 5 syllables in the third line
5. origami—the art of folding paper into the shapes of animals or other objects
6. bonsai—the process of creating very small trees
7. tofu—soybean curd cake that is mixed into many different dishes
8. sushi—thin slices of raw fish wrapped around cooked rice

Metric Conversion Chart

1 inch = 2.54 centimeters	1 fluid ounce (oz.) = 29.573 milliliters
1 foot = .305 meter	1 cup = .24 liter
1 yard = .914 meter	1 pint = .473 liter
1 mile = 1.61 kilometers	1 teaspoon = 4.93 milliliters